Chapter 1: The Kitchen Table Mindset

Embracing the Entrepreneurial Spirit

Embracing the entrepreneurial spirit is essential for anyone looking to transition from a traditional job to running a business from their kitchen table. This spirit embodies the drive to innovate, the willingness to take risks, and the resilience to face challenges head-on. For aspiring entrepreneurs in niches such as digital marketing, e-commerce, or freelancing, fostering this mindset can lead to significant breakthroughs. It's important to recognize that the journey of entrepreneurship is not just about financial gain; it's also about pursuing your passions and creating a fulfilling lifestyle that aligns with your personal and professional goals.

One of the key aspects of embracing this spirit is the ability to identify and harness your unique passions and skills. Whether you have a knack for crafting handmade goods, a passion for teaching through online coaching, or expertise in digital marketing, understanding what drives you will help you carve out a niche in the competitive online marketplace. Taking the time to evaluate your strengths can serve as a foundation for developing your business idea and establishing a brand that resonates with your target audience. This self-awareness is crucial as it will guide your decisions and strategies moving forward.

Another vital element is cultivating a mindset geared towards continuous learning and adaptation. The landscape of online business is ever-evolving, particularly in areas like e-commerce and digital marketing. Entrepreneurs must stay informed about emerging trends and technologies that could impact their business. Embracing a growth mindset enables you to pivot when necessary and seize opportunities that arise. This could mean investing time in online courses, attending webinars, or joining communities of like-minded individuals who can offer support and insights. The more knowledge you acquire, the better equipped you will be to make informed decisions that promote growth and sustainability in your business.

Networking and collaboration play a significant role in embracing the entrepreneurial spirit as well. Building relationships with other entrepreneurs can lead to valuable partnerships and opportunities for collaboration. Engaging with fellow moms who are also navigating the world of remote business can provide a support system that is invaluable during challenging times. Sharing experiences, resources, and tips can foster a sense of community that not only motivates but also opens doors to new possibilities. By leveraging these connections, you can expand your reach, improve your skills, and enhance your overall business acumen.

Lastly, embracing the entrepreneurial spirit requires a proactive approach to overcoming obstacles. Challenges are an inherent part of running a business, whether it's managing time effectively, balancing family responsibilities, or navigating the complexities of online marketing. Developing resilience and a problem-solving mindset can turn setbacks into stepping stones for growth. Establishing productive habits and utilizing productivity hacks can help maintain focus and efficiency in your daily operations. By facing challenges with determination and creativity, you can build a robust business that thrives in the dynamic landscape of the digital world.

Overcoming Fear and Doubt

Fear and doubt are common barriers that many aspiring entrepreneurs face when transitioning from a traditional job to running a business from home. The prospect of leaving the stability of a cubicle can evoke anxiety about financial security, personal skills, and the unknown challenges of entrepreneurship. However, acknowledging these fears is the first step toward overcoming them. It's essential to understand that fear is a natural response, and by addressing it head-on, you can transform it into a powerful motivator that drives you to take action.

One effective strategy for overcoming fear and doubt is to create a clear, actionable plan. Start by setting specific, measurable goals for your business, whether that's launching an e-commerce store, starting a blog, or offering freelance services. Break these goals down into smaller, manageable tasks that you can tackle daily or weekly. This approach not only provides direction but also helps to build your confidence as you accomplish each step. Celebrate these small wins, as they reinforce your belief in your ability to succeed and diminish feelings of doubt over time.

Another crucial aspect of overcoming fear is seeking support from like-minded individuals or communities. Surrounding yourself with fellow entrepreneurs can provide encouragement and practical advice. Join online forums, social media groups, or local meetups focused on home-based businesses. Sharing your experiences and challenges with others who are on a similar journey can help normalize your fears and provide insights on how to navigate them. Additionally, mentorship can play a significant role in alleviating doubts, as experienced entrepreneurs can offer guidance and reassurance based on their own journeys.

Education and skill development are also vital in combating fear and self-doubt. Invest time in learning the necessary skills for your business, whether it's digital marketing, e-commerce strategies, or product creation. Online courses, webinars, and workshops can provide you with the knowledge needed to feel competent and assured in your abilities. As you become more knowledgeable, you'll find that many of your fears stem from a lack of understanding, which can be easily remedied through education and practice.

Lastly, adopt a mindset of resilience and adaptability. Understand that setbacks and failures are part of the entrepreneurial journey. Instead of viewing these challenges as reasons to give up, see them as opportunities for growth and learning. Each obstacle you face will equip you with valuable insights and skills that contribute to your overall success. By reframing your perspective on fear and doubt, you can cultivate a more positive outlook that empowers you to take bold steps toward turning your passion into a profitable e-business from your kitchen table.

Setting Realistic Goals

Setting realistic goals is crucial for anyone looking to transition from a traditional job to running a business from their kitchen table. The excitement of starting your own venture can sometimes cloud your judgment, leading to lofty ambitions that may not align with your current resources or skills. Begin by assessing your capabilities and the time you can realistically dedicate to your new business. This self-evaluation serves as the foundation for setting achievable goals that can guide your efforts without overwhelming you.

When establishing your goals, consider employing the SMART criteria: Specific, Measurable, Achievable, Relevant, and Time-bound. A specific goal might be to launch an online course on a subject you're passionate about, rather than a vague intention to "start a business." By making your objectives measurable, you can track your progress, such as aiming for a certain number of students enrolled within six months. Ensuring your goals are achievable helps prevent burnout and frustration, while relevance guarantees that your goals align with your overall vision for leaving the cubicle behind.

Breaking down larger goals into smaller, manageable tasks is an effective strategy that keeps you motivated. For instance, if your aim is to generate passive income through an e-commerce platform, start by dedicating one week to researching products, another week to setting up your store, and subsequent weeks to marketing your offerings. This incremental approach not only makes the process less daunting but also allows you to celebrate small victories along the way, reinforcing your commitment to the journey.

Time management is another critical aspect of setting realistic goals. As a home-based entrepreneur, distractions can easily derail your plans. Establish a timeline for each goal and allocate specific time slots dedicated to working on your business. Use tools like calendars or project management software to visualize your tasks and deadlines. This structured approach helps maintain focus and ensures that you make consistent progress toward your objectives.

Finally, remain flexible and open to reevaluating your goals as you gain more experience in your venture. The landscape of online business is constantly evolving, and what seemed like a realistic target six months ago may no longer be relevant. Regularly assess your progress and be willing to adjust your goals based on new insights, market trends, or personal circumstances. This adaptability will not only help you stay on track but also foster a mindset that embraces growth and resilience, essential traits for any successful entrepreneur operating from their kitchen table.

Chapter 2: Discovering Your Passion

Identifying Your Skills and Interests

Identifying your skills and interests is a crucial first step when transitioning from a traditional job to running a business from your kitchen table. This process not only helps you understand what you enjoy doing but also highlights the unique abilities you possess that can translate into a viable business model. To begin, take stock of your past experiences, both professional and personal. Consider the tasks that excited you in previous roles, hobbies you are passionate about, and any skills you have developed over time. This self-assessment will provide a solid foundation for determining which avenues to explore further.

Once you have a comprehensive list of your skills and interests, it's important to analyze how they intersect with potential market opportunities. For instance, if you enjoy crafting and have a talent for design, you might consider starting an e-commerce store to sell handmade goods. Alternatively, if you possess strong writing skills and a knack for digital marketing, you could explore freelance opportunities or even start a blog focused on your areas of expertise. Research various niches to identify where your interests align with market demand, allowing you to carve out a unique space in the competitive online landscape.

Networking with others in your desired field can also play a significant role in identifying your skills and interests. Engaging with fellow entrepreneurs, joining online communities, or attending local meetups can provide valuable insights into what is working for others. These interactions can help you refine your ideas and discover new inspirations that you may not have considered before. Additionally, mentorship from experienced professionals can guide you in recognizing your strengths and applying them effectively in a business context.

As you delve deeper into your self-discovery process, consider taking personality and skills assessments. Tools like the Myers-Briggs Type Indicator or StrengthsFinder can provide a clearer understanding of your innate strengths and preferences. This quantitative data, combined with your qualitative reflections, will allow you to make informed decisions about the types of business ventures that might best suit you. Remember, the goal is to find a balance between what you love to do and what can be monetized effectively.

Finally, be prepared to adapt your initial ideas as you gain more clarity about your skills and interests. The journey of starting a business is often filled with unexpected twists and turns, and flexibility is key to finding success. Embrace the process of exploration and experimentation, as this will lead you to discover new passions and refine your business concept. Ultimately, identifying your skills and interests is not just about pinpointing what you want to do; it's about laying the groundwork for a fulfilling and profitable venture that resonates with your personal values and lifestyle goals.

Market Research: Finding Your Niche

Market research is a crucial step in finding your niche, especially when transitioning from a traditional job to running a business from your kitchen table. It allows you to understand the landscape of your chosen market, identify potential customers, and analyze competitors. To begin, start by defining your interests and skills. Reflect on what excites you and where your expertise lies. This self-assessment will help you narrow down ideas that not only align with your passion but also have the potential for profitability.

Next, gather data on your target audience. Utilize online tools and resources to create customer profiles. Who are they? What are their needs and pain points? Platforms like social media, forums, and surveys can provide valuable insights into customer preferences and behaviors. By understanding your audience, you can tailor your offerings to meet their specific demands, ensuring that your business resonates with them on a deeper level.

Competitor analysis is another critical component of market research. Identify key players in your niche and examine their strengths and weaknesses. What do they offer that attracts customers? What gaps exist in their services or products that you could fill? By analyzing competitors, you can develop a unique selling proposition that sets your business apart. This approach not only positions you effectively in the market but also enhances your ability to capture the attention of potential customers.

Once you've gathered data about your audience and competitors, it's time to validate your ideas. Consider conducting small-scale tests, such as launching a minimal viable product or offering a pilot service. Collect feedback from your early users to understand what works and what doesn't. This iterative process allows you to refine your offerings based on real-world insights, ultimately increasing your chances of success as you transition into a full-scale operation.

Finally, keep in mind that market research is an ongoing process. As trends and consumer preferences evolve, staying attuned to shifts in the market is essential. Regularly updating your research will help you adapt your strategies and offerings, ensuring that you remain relevant and competitive. By committing to this continuous learning approach, you can confidently navigate the challenges of running a profitable e-business from your kitchen table, transforming your passion into a sustainable livelihood.

Validating Your Business Idea

Validating your business idea is a crucial step in transitioning from a traditional job to running your own venture from your kitchen table. This process involves assessing the viability of your concept before investing time and resources. To begin, conduct thorough market research to identify your target audience and understand their needs. Utilize surveys, interviews, and social media interactions to gather insights. This information will help you determine whether your idea addresses a genuine problem or fulfills a specific desire, which is essential for attracting potential customers.

Once you have a clear understanding of your target market, consider creating a Minimum Viable Product (MVP). An MVP is a simplified version of your product or service that allows you to test your concept with real users without extensive development. For instance, if you plan to sell handmade goods online, start by offering a small selection of items to gauge interest. This approach enables you to gather feedback and make necessary adjustments before fully launching your business, ensuring that you align your offerings with customer preferences.

Another effective method for validating your business idea is to analyze the competition. Research existing businesses within your niche to see how they operate, what they offer, and how they attract customers. This analysis will not only reveal market gaps you can fill but also provide insights into successful strategies you can adapt. By understanding what works for others, you can refine your own approach and differentiate yourself in the crowded e-commerce landscape.

Engaging with potential customers through social media platforms and online forums can further validate your business idea. Create content that resonates with your target audience and encourages discussion. By observing their reactions and feedback, you can gain valuable insights into their preferences and pain points. This engagement will also help you build a community around your brand, fostering loyalty and trust even before your official launch.

Lastly, consider leveraging online tools and platforms that can help you validate your ideas. Websites like Kickstarter or Indiegogo allow entrepreneurs to present concepts and gauge interest through crowdfunding. By promoting your idea and measuring the response, you can determine whether there is a market for your product or service. This approach not only validates your business idea but also provides an opportunity to raise initial funds, setting the stage for a successful kitchen table hustle.

Chapter 3: Kindle Boom

Writing Your First eBook

Writing your first eBook can be a transformative step in launching your home-based business, especially in the era of the Kindle Boom. With the growth of e-reader technology, self-publishing has become an accessible avenue for entrepreneurs looking to share their expertise and monetize their passions. The first step in this journey is to identify a niche that aligns with your skills and interests. Whether you're focused on digital marketing, freelancing, or crafting, selecting a topic that resonates with your audience is essential for capturing their attention and driving sales.

Once you've pinpointed your niche, outline your eBook by breaking down your subject into manageable sections. This structure will serve as a roadmap, guiding your writing process and ensuring you cover all necessary points. For instance, if your niche is remote business strategies for moms, you might divide your eBook into sections on time management, effective communication, and balancing family life with entrepreneurial endeavors. A clear outline not only keeps you organized but also helps maintain a logical flow that readers will appreciate.

As you begin to write, establish a consistent routine that allows you to focus on your project without distractions. Set aside dedicated time each day or week, treating your writing sessions as crucial appointments. This discipline is vital, especially for those working from home, where interruptions can be frequent. Remember that writing is a process; don't strive for perfection in your first draft. Instead, focus on getting your ideas down, knowing you can refine them later.

Editing is a critical phase in creating a polished eBook. Once your draft is complete, take the time to review and revise your work thoroughly. Look for clarity, coherence, and conciseness. It's often helpful to have a trusted friend or colleague read through your manuscript to provide feedback. They can offer a fresh perspective and catch errors you might have overlooked. Additionally, consider hiring a professional editor to ensure your eBook meets high standards, which is particularly important in a competitive market.

Finally, once your eBook is ready for publication, leverage digital marketing strategies to promote it effectively. Utilize social media platforms, email newsletters, and blogging to reach your target audience. Craft compelling content that highlights the value of your eBook and encourages potential readers to make a purchase. Creating an engaging landing page with testimonials and sneak peeks can also enhance your promotional efforts. By following these steps, you can successfully launch your first eBook and take a significant leap toward achieving your goal of running a profitable business from your kitchen table.

Formatting and Publishing on Kindle

Formatting your manuscript correctly is crucial when publishing on Kindle. Amazon's Kindle Direct Publishing (KDP) platform offers specific formatting guidelines that ensure your book appears professional and is easy to read. Start by using tools like Microsoft Word or Scrivener, which allow you to set up proper styles for headings, paragraphs, and lists. Pay attention to font choices and sizes, and ensure that your text is free of unnecessary formatting, such as excessive bold or italicized text. Proper formatting not only enhances the reading experience but also increases the chances of your book being accepted during the publishing process.

Once you've formatted your manuscript, it's time to convert it into a Kindle-compatible format. Amazon recommends using the MOBI format for your eBook, but KDP also accepts DOC/DOCX, HTML, and EPUB files. Tools like Calibre or Kindle Create can help you convert your document easily. After conversion, preview your book using the Kindle Previewer tool to see how it will look on various Kindle devices and apps. This step is essential to catch any formatting errors or inconsistencies before your book goes live.

Cover design is another critical element of publishing on Kindle. Your book cover is often the first impression potential readers will have, so it needs to be eye-catching and professional. Consider hiring a graphic designer or using platforms like Canva, which offer user-friendly templates specifically for book covers. Make sure your cover design aligns with the genre and theme of your book, as this helps attract the right audience. Remember that the cover must be at least 1,000 pixels in height and 625 pixels in width to ensure quality on all devices.

After your manuscript is formatted and your cover is designed, you can begin the publishing process on KDP. Create an account on the KDP platform and fill in the required information about your book, including the title, author name, and description. Choose your keywords and categories wisely, as these will determine how easily readers can find your book. Set your pricing strategy, considering factors like book length and market competition. KDP allows you to choose between a 35% or 70% royalty option depending on your pricing and distribution choices.

Finally, once your book is published, focus on marketing it effectively. Utilize social media platforms, email newsletters, and blogging to promote your eBook. Engage with your audience by offering insights related to your book's content and sharing your journey as a kitchen table entrepreneur. Consider running promotional campaigns, such as free or discounted days, to increase visibility and attract reviews. Building a solid marketing strategy will help you reach your target audience and drive sales, turning your passion project into a profitable venture from the comfort of your kitchen table.

Marketing Your eBook for Success

To successfully market your eBook, it is essential to identify your target audience and understand their needs. Knowing who you are writing for will help you tailor your marketing strategies to reach the right people. For instance, if your eBook focuses on productivity hacks for home business owners, you should engage with communities that prioritize efficiency and time management. Utilize social media platforms, forums, and groups where your potential readers gather to share insights, ask questions, and seek advice. This targeted approach ensures that your marketing efforts resonate with those who will benefit most from your content.

Creating a strong online presence is crucial for eBook success. Start by developing a professional website or blog that showcases your expertise and the value of your eBook. Use engaging content, such as blog posts related to your eBook's topic, to draw in your audience and establish your authority in the niche. Incorporate search engine optimization (SEO) techniques to improve your site's visibility in search results. The more traffic you attract, the greater the chances of converting visitors into eBook buyers.

Leveraging social media is another effective way to promote your eBook. Choose platforms where your target audience is most active and create compelling posts that highlight the benefits of your eBook. Use eye-catching graphics, quotes, and short excerpts to entice potential readers. Engage with your audience by responding to comments, asking for feedback, and creating polls to foster a sense of community. Building relationships with your followers will encourage them to share your content and help you reach a wider audience.

Consider implementing email marketing as a powerful tool for promoting your eBook. Build an email list by offering a free resource related to your eBook topic, such as a checklist or a mini-guide. Use this list to send out regular updates, insights, and promotional offers. Craft well-written emails that provide value and encourage readers to purchase your eBook. Personalization in your email campaigns can significantly enhance engagement and conversion rates, making your marketing efforts more effective.

Lastly, explore collaborations and partnerships to expand your reach. Connect with other authors, bloggers, or influencers in your niche who share a similar audience. Guest blogging, co-hosting webinars, or participating in online events can introduce your eBook to new readers. Consider offering affiliate programs to incentivize others to promote your eBook, creating a win-win situation for both parties. By combining these strategies, you can build a robust marketing plan that maximizes your eBook's visibility and sales potential.

Chapter 4: Remote Business Strategies for Moms

Balancing Family and Entrepreneurship

Balancing family and entrepreneurship is a challenge many aspiring business owners face, especially when working from home. The allure of starting a profitable e-business from your kitchen table often comes with the complexities of managing family responsibilities alongside business growth. Establishing a clear boundary between work and family time is essential. This can be achieved by setting specific work hours that align with your family's schedule, thus allowing you to dedicate focused time to both your business and your loved ones.

Prioritization plays a crucial role in maintaining this balance. As a home-based entrepreneur, you may find yourself juggling various tasks, from digital marketing to customer service. To manage these effectively, create a daily or weekly priority list. Identify key tasks that will drive your business forward and allocate time slots for family activities. This structured approach not only keeps your business organized but also ensures that family quality time is protected, fostering a supportive home environment.

Utilizing technology can greatly enhance your ability to balance these aspects of your life. Tools such as project management software, calendar applications, and communication platforms streamline your work processes, allowing you to maximize productivity during designated work hours. By automating certain tasks and delegating responsibilities where possible, you can free up valuable time to spend with your family, ensuring that neither your business nor your loved ones feel neglected.

Moreover, involving your family in your entrepreneurial journey can create a sense of unity and shared purpose. Encourage family members to contribute ideas or assist with aspects of the business that match their interests or skills. This not only strengthens family bonds but also brings fresh perspectives to your business. By fostering a collaborative environment, you can transform what might be seen as a burden into an enriching experience that benefits both your professional and personal life.

Lastly, self-care should not be overlooked in the pursuit of balancing family and entrepreneurship. Taking time for yourself is essential for maintaining your mental and emotional well-being. Engaging in activities that recharge your energy, whether through exercise, hobbies, or quiet time, can enhance your productivity and creativity. Remember, a healthy balance between family and business is not merely about managing time; it's about nurturing relationships and personal fulfillment that empower you to thrive in both domains.

Time Management Techniques

Time management is a crucial skill for anyone looking to transition from a traditional job to running a business from home. For aspiring entrepreneurs, especially those in the Kindle Boom and other home-based ventures, effective time management can mean the difference between success and stagnation. One of the most effective techniques is prioritization. Identifying the most critical tasks that align with your business goals ensures that your time is spent on activities that drive results. Using tools like the Eisenhower Matrix can help clarify which tasks are urgent versus important, allowing you to focus your energy on what truly matters.

Another valuable technique is the Pomodoro Technique, which encourages work in focused intervals followed by short breaks. This method not only boosts productivity but also combats mental fatigue. For home-based entrepreneurs, distractions can be plentiful—children, household chores, and the allure of leisure activities can easily disrupt focus. By committing to intense, timed work sessions, you can create a rhythm that maximizes your output while maintaining your mental well-being.

Setting specific goals and deadlines is another powerful time management technique. When you have clear objectives, it becomes much easier to allocate your time effectively. Break larger projects into smaller, manageable tasks and assign realistic deadlines to each. This not only helps in tracking progress but also provides a sense of accomplishment as you complete each task. Utilizing project management tools can streamline this process, making it simpler to visualize your workload and stay on track.

Additionally, creating a structured daily routine can significantly enhance productivity. Establishing designated work hours helps to separate your personal life from your professional tasks, reducing the likelihood of burnout. For those managing family responsibilities alongside their business, incorporating family time into your schedule can create balance and ensure that both personal and professional commitments are met. Consistency in your daily routine builds momentum and makes it easier to stay focused on your entrepreneurial goals.

Lastly, leveraging technology can greatly enhance your time management efforts. Various apps and tools are designed to help you organize your tasks, set reminders, and track time spent on different activities. Whether you're managing a blog, selling handmade goods, or offering online coaching, integrating these digital solutions can optimize your workflow and free up more time for creative pursuits. As you implement these time management techniques, you'll find that you not only gain control over your schedule but also enhance your overall productivity, allowing you to turn your kitchen table hustle into a thriving e-business.

Creating a Support Network

Creating a support network is essential for anyone looking to transition from a traditional job to running a business from their kitchen table, especially in the dynamic landscape of the digital economy. A support network can provide not only emotional backing but also practical resources, insights, and opportunities that can propel your business forward. Building this network involves connecting with like-minded individuals, mentors, and resources that align with your entrepreneurial goals.

Start by tapping into online communities that cater to your specific niche. Social media platforms, forums, and dedicated websites are treasure troves of information and support. Engage in discussions, ask questions, and share your experiences. Platforms like Facebook Groups and LinkedIn can offer a sense of camaraderie as you connect with other home-based entrepreneurs who understand the unique challenges and joys of running a business from home. These connections can lead to collaborations, partnerships, and even lifelong friendships.

Mentorship plays a pivotal role in the development of a successful support network. Seek out individuals who have successfully navigated the transition from corporate life to entrepreneurship. These mentors can provide invaluable guidance, share their experiences, and offer advice tailored to your specific challenges. Consider reaching out to local business organizations or online mentorship programs that specialize in supporting home-based entrepreneurs. Having someone to turn to for advice can make a significant difference as you face the ups and downs of building your e-business.

Networking events, both virtual and in-person, can also enhance your support network. These gatherings offer opportunities to meet other entrepreneurs, learn from industry experts, and share your own insights. Look for workshops, webinars, and local meetups focused on digital marketing, e-commerce, or specific niches like handmade goods or online coaching. Engaging with others in these settings can lead to new connections and potential collaborations that can expand your reach and resources.

Finally, consider creating or joining accountability groups. These small groups of entrepreneurs can meet regularly to discuss goals, progress, and challenges. The accountability provided by peers can motivate you to stay focused and push through obstacles. Sharing your victories and setbacks with others who are in the same boat can foster a sense of community and support. By actively participating in these groups, you contribute to a culture of encouragement and resource-sharing that benefits everyone involved.

Chapter 5: Digital Marketing for Home-Based Entrepreneurs

Building Your Online Presence

Building your online presence is a crucial step for anyone looking to transition from a traditional job to running a profitable e-business from home. Establishing a strong online presence not only helps you connect with your target audience but also boosts your credibility in the increasingly competitive digital marketplace. The first step in this journey is creating a professional website that serves as your central hub. Your website should reflect your brand identity, showcase your products or services, and provide valuable content that resonates with your niche. Consider using user-friendly platforms like WordPress or Shopify to get started, ensuring that your site is mobile-responsive and optimized for search engines.

Once your website is up and running, leverage social media platforms to amplify your reach. Identify which platforms your target audience frequents the most, whether it's Facebook, Instagram, Pinterest, or LinkedIn, and create profiles that align with your brand. Share engaging content, such as tips related to your niche, behind-the-scenes glimpses of your business, and personal stories that illustrate your journey. Regularly interact with your followers by responding to comments and messages, which helps build a community around your brand and fosters loyalty among your audience.

Content marketing is another vital component of building your online presence. Start a blog on your website where you can share valuable insights, tutorials, and resources related to your niche. This not only positions you as an authority in your field but also drives organic traffic to your site. Optimize your blog posts with relevant keywords to improve your search engine rankings. Additionally, consider guest blogging on other reputable sites to expand your reach and attract new visitors to your website. Each piece of content you create is an opportunity to connect with potential customers and showcase your expertise.

Email marketing is an effective tool for nurturing relationships with your audience. Create a mailing list by offering a freebie, such as an e-book or a checklist, in exchange for email addresses. Regularly send out newsletters featuring valuable content, exclusive offers, and updates about your business. Personalize your emails to make your subscribers feel valued, and segment your list to tailor your messages based on their interests or behaviors. By maintaining consistent communication, you can keep your audience engaged and encourage them to become loyal customers.

Lastly, consider exploring online communities and forums related to your niche. Engaging in these spaces allows you to connect with like-minded individuals, share your expertise, and promote your business. Platforms such as Facebook groups, Reddit, or specialized forums provide opportunities to answer questions, offer advice, and showcase your products or services subtly. Building relationships within these communities can lead to valuable collaborations and referrals, further enhancing your online presence. By combining these strategies, you can effectively build a robust online presence that supports your journey as a home-based entrepreneur.

Social Media Marketing Strategies

Social media marketing has become an essential tool for anyone looking to turn their passions into a profitable e-business. For those leaving the cubicle behind and starting their ventures from their kitchen tables, harnessing the power of platforms like Facebook, Instagram, and Pinterest can significantly boost visibility and engagement. Understanding which platforms align best with your target audience is the first step in crafting an effective social media strategy. For instance, visual products, such as handmade crafts or e-books, may thrive on platforms like Instagram and Pinterest, where imagery can captivate potential customers.

Creating a consistent brand voice across social media channels is crucial. This involves defining your brand's personality and ensuring that all content shared reflects that identity. Whether your brand is playful, professional, or nurturing, consistency helps to build trust and recognition. Utilizing a content calendar can aid in planning posts that align with your brand's voice, ensuring that you maintain a steady stream of content that resonates with your audience, whether they are moms seeking remote business strategies or aspiring online coaches.

Engagement is another cornerstone of successful social media marketing. Simply posting content is not enough; interacting with your audience fosters a community around your brand. Responding to comments, participating in discussions, and asking for feedback can create a loyal following and encourage word-of-mouth referrals. Additionally, consider hosting live sessions or Q&As to connect with your audience on a more personal level, which can be particularly effective for online coaching or consulting services.

Paid advertising on social media can also amplify your reach and accelerate growth. Platforms like Facebook and Instagram offer targeted advertising options that allow you to reach specific demographics aligned with your business. Investing in ads can be a game-changer for kitchen table startups seeking to expand their audience. By carefully crafting ad content and targeting the right audience segments, you can drive traffic to your website or e-commerce store and increase sales.

Lastly, measuring the effectiveness of your social media efforts is vital for ongoing improvement. Utilizing analytics tools provided by social media platforms can help you track engagement, reach, and conversion rates. By analyzing this data, you can adjust your strategies to focus on what works best for your business. This continuous cycle of testing and adaptation will not only enhance your social media presence but also contribute to the overall success of your e-business, paving the way for long-term profitability.

Email Marketing Essentials

Email marketing remains one of the most effective tools for home-based entrepreneurs seeking to engage with customers and drive sales. For those leaving their traditional jobs behind and setting up businesses from their kitchen tables, understanding how to harness the power of email marketing is essential. This involves building a targeted email list that consists of individuals who have shown interest in your products or services. Start by offering valuable content or incentives, such as free resources or discounts, in exchange for email sign-ups. This not only grows your list but also establishes a foundation of potential customers who are eager to hear from you.

Once you have developed your email list, crafting compelling content is crucial. This means creating messages that resonate with your audience, whether you are selling handmade goods, offering coaching services, or sharing tips for productivity. Personalization is key; address your subscribers by name and segment your audience based on their preferences or behaviors. This allows you to tailor your messages, increasing the likelihood that they will engage with your content and take action, whether it's making a purchase or sharing your email with others.

Consistency in your email marketing efforts is just as important as the content itself. Establishing a regular schedule for sending emails helps keep your business top of mind for your subscribers. Whether you choose to send weekly newsletters, promotional offers, or educational content, maintaining a predictable rhythm builds trust and anticipation among your audience. It's also beneficial to track performance metrics such as open rates, click-through rates, and conversion rates. These insights provide valuable feedback, allowing you to refine your strategies and improve future campaigns.

Moreover, effective email marketing should include clear calls-to-action (CTAs) that guide your subscribers toward the next steps you want them to take. Whether it's visiting your online store, booking a consultation, or following you on social media, strong CTAs can significantly enhance engagement. Make sure these actions are easy to complete and visually stand out within your emails. Additionally, consider incorporating A/B testing to evaluate which CTAs resonate more with your audience, enabling you to optimize your approach over time.

Finally, remember that building a successful email marketing strategy is an ongoing process that requires adaptation and growth. As your business evolves, so too should your email marketing tactics. Stay informed about the latest trends and best practices in digital marketing to ensure that your strategy remains relevant and effective. By continually refining your approach and staying connected with your audience, you can maximize the potential of email marketing as a powerful tool to support your kitchen table hustle.

Chapter 6: E-commerce Tips for Kitchen Table Startups

Setting Up Your Online Store

Setting up your online store is a crucial step in transforming your passion into a profitable business. The first thing to consider is choosing the right platform that aligns with your products and target audience. Options like Shopify, WooCommerce, and Etsy cater to different needs, from fully customizable storefronts to user-friendly interfaces for handmade goods. Research each platform's features, fees, and scalability to ensure it meets your requirements as you begin your journey. Take into account your level of technical expertise, as some platforms may require more hands-on management than others.

Once you've selected a platform, it's essential to design your store's layout and aesthetics. Your online store should reflect your brand identity and appeal to your target customers. Use high-quality images, consistent color schemes, and easy-to-navigate menus to create an inviting shopping experience. Consider the user journey from landing on your site to completing a purchase. A well-structured site can significantly reduce bounce rates and increase conversion rates, so pay attention to details like product descriptions and category organization.

Next, focus on product listings. High-quality photographs and compelling descriptions are essential for attracting and converting visitors into buyers. Ensure that your images showcase your products from multiple angles and in various settings to provide customers with a clear understanding of what they are purchasing. Write engaging descriptions that highlight the unique features and benefits of your products, incorporating keywords that improve search engine visibility. This not only helps customers make informed decisions but also boosts your store's SEO, making it easier for potential buyers to find you online.

Payment processing and inventory management are also critical components of your online store setup. Choose a reliable payment gateway that offers multiple payment options to accommodate various customer preferences. Security is paramount; ensure your chosen service complies with current safety standards to protect customer information. Additionally, implement an inventory management system that tracks your stock levels in real-time, helping you avoid overselling or running out of popular items. This organization will streamline your operations and enhance customer satisfaction.

Finally, don't forget about marketing your online store once it's up and running. Utilize social media platforms, email marketing, and content marketing to reach your target audience effectively. Create engaging content that resonates with your customer base, showcasing your products and sharing your personal story as a kitchen table entrepreneur. Building an online community around your brand fosters trust and loyalty, increasing the likelihood of repeat business. As you establish your presence, continually analyze your performance metrics and adjust your strategies to ensure sustained growth and success in the competitive e-commerce landscape.

Choosing the Right E-commerce Platform

When embarking on your journey to establish an e-commerce business from your kitchen table, choosing the right platform is a crucial step that can significantly impact your success. The e-commerce platform serves as the foundation of your online store, facilitating transactions, managing inventory, and providing a user-friendly experience for your customers. With numerous options available, it's essential to evaluate each platform based on your specific needs, budget, and technical expertise.

First, consider the type of products you plan to sell. Some platforms cater better to specific niches, such as handmade goods, digital products, or subscription services. For instance, if you're focused on crafting and selling handmade goods, platforms like Etsy may offer tailored features that align with your goals. Conversely, if you intend to sell digital products or offer coaching services, platforms like Shopify or WooCommerce could provide the flexibility and scalability required for your business model.

Next, examine the ease of use and level of technical knowledge required for each platform. Many entrepreneurs starting from their kitchen tables may not have extensive technical skills. Therefore, selecting a platform with a user-friendly interface can save you time and frustration. Look for options that offer drag-and-drop functionalities and customizable templates, enabling you to create a professional-looking store without needing to code. Additionally, consider the availability of customer support, as having access to assistance can be invaluable when navigating challenges.

Another important factor is the payment processing capabilities of the e-commerce platform. Ensure that the platform you choose supports multiple payment methods to accommodate a broader range of customers. Consider transaction fees, as these can vary significantly between platforms and can affect your profit margins. Platforms like PayPal and Stripe are commonly integrated into many e-commerce solutions and provide secure payment options that enhance customer trust.

Lastly, think about the long-term growth potential of the platform. As your business expands, you may want to explore additional features such as built-in analytics, marketing tools, and the ability to integrate with other software. A scalable platform will allow you to add functionalities as your needs evolve, ensuring that your e-commerce store can grow alongside your ambitions. Conduct thorough research, read reviews, and even seek advice from other home-based entrepreneurs to find the platform that aligns best with your vision and operational requirements.

Effective Product Listings and Descriptions

Effective product listings and descriptions are crucial for anyone looking to succeed in the competitive world of e-commerce, particularly for those running a business from their kitchen table. A well-crafted product listing serves as the first point of contact between your potential customers and your offerings. It is essential to convey the value and benefits of your products clearly and compellingly. This involves not only showcasing the features but also addressing the needs and desires of your target audience. Understanding who your ideal customer is can help you tailor your listings to resonate with them, ultimately driving more sales.

When creating product descriptions, it is vital to use engaging and descriptive language that paints a vivid picture of what you are selling. Instead of simply listing specifications, tell a story that connects with your audience emotionally. Highlight how your product can solve a problem or enhance their lives, making it relatable. Use sensory details that allow customers to envision the experience of using your product, whether it's the texture of a handmade item or the convenience of a digital tool. This approach not only captures attention but also builds a connection that can lead to conversions.

In addition to the written content, incorporating high-quality images plays a significant role in effective product listings. Visuals can often communicate what words cannot, offering a clear representation of your product. Make sure to use multiple images that showcase different angles and uses of the product. If applicable, consider including lifestyle images that demonstrate the product in a real-life setting. This can help potential buyers visualize how the product fits into their daily lives, further encouraging them to make a purchase.

SEO (Search Engine Optimization) is another critical aspect of product listings that should not be overlooked. By incorporating relevant keywords into your product titles and descriptions, you increase the chances of your listings appearing in search results, both on e-commerce platforms and search engines. Researching which keywords your target audience is using can give you a competitive edge. However, it's essential to strike a balance between optimizing for search engines and maintaining readable, customer-friendly descriptions.

Finally, don't underestimate the power of customer reviews and testimonials in your product listings. Social proof can significantly influence purchasing decisions, as potential buyers often look for validation from others before committing to a purchase. Encourage satisfied customers to leave positive feedback and display these reviews prominently in your listings. This not only builds trust but also enhances your credibility as a seller, making it easier to convert curious visitors into loyal customers. By focusing on these elements, you can create effective product listings and descriptions that drive sales and foster long-term success for your kitchen table business.

Chapter 7: Productivity Hacks for Home Business Owners

Creating a Distraction-Free Workspace

Creating a distraction-free workspace is essential for anyone looking to turn their passion into a profitable e-business from the comfort of their kitchen table. A well-organized and focused environment can significantly enhance productivity, especially for individuals transitioning from traditional office settings to remote work. The first step in establishing this kind of workspace is to designate a specific area solely for your business activities. This could be a corner of your kitchen, a spare room, or even a nook in your living room. By assigning a particular space for work, you create a physical boundary that helps mentally separate business tasks from personal life.

Once you have designated your workspace, it is crucial to minimize distractions within that area. Start by decluttering your desk and removing any items that do not contribute to your work. Keep only the essentials within arm's reach, such as your laptop, notepads, and necessary tools for your specific business. Consider using storage solutions, like baskets or drawer organizers, to keep everything tidy. Additionally, if possible, inform family members or roommates of your work hours to establish boundaries and minimize interruptions. This communication is especially important for moms balancing home duties while trying to run a business.

Another effective strategy for maintaining a distraction-free environment is to control external noise. Depending on your living situation, noise can be a significant barrier to concentration. Consider investing in noise-canceling headphones or playing soft background music to help drown out distractions. If your workspace is in a noisy area of the home, you might also explore soundproofing options, such as heavy curtains or rugs, to absorb sound. Creating an environment conducive to focus will enable you to dive deeper into your tasks and maintain a flow state, enhancing both creativity and productivity.

Lighting plays a critical role in your workspace's atmosphere and can significantly impact your ability to concentrate. Natural light is ideal, as it can improve mood and energy levels. If possible, position your workspace near a window to benefit from daylight. When natural light isn't available, ensure that your workspace is well-lit with soft, adjustable lighting that reduces eye strain. The right lighting can help you feel more alert and engaged in your work, ultimately leading to higher productivity and better results in your e-business endeavors.

Lastly, consider the importance of comfort in your workspace. A comfortable chair and desk setup can make a world of difference in terms of focus and productivity. Ergonomic furniture can prevent discomfort during long hours of work, allowing you to maintain your concentration on business tasks. Additionally, personalizing your workspace with inspiring quotes, plants, or meaningful objects can foster a positive and motivating environment. By thoughtfully designing a distraction-free workspace, you set the stage for success, enabling you to transform your kitchen table hustle into a thriving e-business.

Tools and Apps for Increased Efficiency

In the fast-paced world of online business, leveraging the right tools and apps can significantly enhance efficiency and productivity for home-based entrepreneurs. With various niches like digital marketing, e-commerce, and freelancing, the options available can feel overwhelming. However, identifying and utilizing the most effective tools tailored to your specific needs can streamline operations and help maintain focus on growth. This subchapter will explore essential tools and applications that can elevate your Kitchen Table Hustle to new heights.

Project management tools such as Trello, Asana, and Monday.com can transform how you organize tasks and collaborate with team members. These platforms allow you to create boards and lists that visualize your workflow, making it easier to track progress and deadlines. For remote business strategies, these tools facilitate seamless communication among team members, ensuring everyone is aligned and accountable for their responsibilities. By breaking down projects into manageable tasks, you can maintain clarity and focus, essential for entrepreneurs juggling multiple roles.

In the realm of digital marketing, analytics and social media management tools are indispensable. Applications like Hootsuite or Buffer enable you to schedule posts across various platforms, ensuring consistent engagement without the need for constant monitoring. Google Analytics provides valuable insights into your website traffic and user behavior, allowing you to refine your strategies and target your audience more effectively. Understanding these metrics is crucial for home-based entrepreneurs, as it helps tailor marketing efforts to maximize reach and conversion rates.

For those venturing into e-commerce or selling handmade goods online, platforms like Shopify, Etsy, and WooCommerce offer user-friendly solutions to set up and manage online stores. These tools not only simplify the process of listing products but also integrate payment processing and inventory management. Additionally, they provide analytics to help track sales trends and customer preferences, which can inform future product offerings. By streamlining these processes, you can focus on creating and marketing your products rather than getting bogged down by logistics.

Lastly, productivity apps such as Focus@Will, Todoist, and Evernote can help maintain personal organization and work-life balance, which is vital for home business owners. Focus@Will offers music designed to enhance concentration, while Todoist allows you to prioritize tasks and set deadlines. Evernote serves as a digital notebook for capturing ideas, notes, and inspirations, keeping your creative juices flowing. Implementing these tools into your daily routine can help you stay organized, minimize distractions, and ultimately, drive your business forward.

By integrating these tools and apps into your workflow, you can create a more efficient and productive environment for your home-based business. Whether you are crafting digital products, providing coaching, or managing an e-commerce site, the right technology can streamline operations and foster growth. Embracing these resources not only saves time but also empowers you to focus on what matters most: turning your passion into a profitable venture from the comfort of your kitchen table.

The Importance of Routine

Establishing a routine is crucial for anyone looking to transition from a traditional job to running a successful e-business from home. The kitchen table, often seen as a casual space, can become a powerhouse of productivity when structured effectively. A well-defined routine helps to create boundaries between personal life and work, which is particularly important for those who may find it challenging to separate the two in a home environment. By setting specific work hours and adhering to them, entrepreneurs can foster a mindset that prioritizes productivity and professionalism.

A consistent routine not only enhances focus but also boosts motivation. When you wake up each day with a clear plan, it sets a tone of purpose and direction. This is especially valuable for remote business strategies aimed at moms juggling household responsibilities alongside their entrepreneurial ventures. By allocating specific times for tasks such as content creation, marketing, or customer engagement, individuals can ensure that they remain committed to their business goals without feeling overwhelmed. This structure is vital for maintaining momentum, particularly in the competitive digital landscape.

Moreover, routines facilitate better time management, which is essential for home-based entrepreneurs. With numerous distractions present in a home setting, having a structured daily schedule allows for efficient allocation of time towards various aspects of the business. For instance, designated blocks for e-commerce activities, like managing an online store or fulfilling orders, can help streamline operations and maximize productivity. Implementing time blocks can also prevent burnout by ensuring that breaks and self-care are integrated into the day, which is crucial for sustaining long-term business health.

Building passive income streams from home requires a combination of consistent effort and strategic planning. A routine that incorporates regular review sessions can help entrepreneurs assess their progress and pivot their strategies as needed. These sessions can include analyzing sales data, evaluating marketing campaigns, or brainstorming new product ideas. By routinely dedicating time to reflect on business performance, home-based entrepreneurs can make informed decisions that enhance their growth potential and adapt to market changes effectively.

Lastly, the importance of routine extends to cultivating a professional mindset, even when working from the kitchen table. By treating your home business with the same seriousness as a traditional job, you reinforce the commitment necessary for success. This includes not only adhering to a structured schedule but also dressing for success, creating a dedicated workspace, and minimizing distractions. These practices help to establish a professional atmosphere that fosters creativity and encourages the entrepreneurial spirit, ultimately leading to a thriving e-business.

Chapter 8: Creating Passive Income Streams from Home

Understanding Passive Income

Understanding passive income is essential for anyone looking to create a sustainable and profitable e-business from the comfort of their kitchen table. Unlike traditional income streams that require continuous effort and time, passive income allows individuals to earn money with minimal ongoing involvement. This concept is particularly appealing to those who wish to leave the cubicle behind and embrace a more flexible lifestyle, especially for busy moms, home-based entrepreneurs, and freelancers. By understanding the various forms of passive income, you can strategically incorporate them into your business model, allowing for greater financial freedom and the opportunity to focus on what you love.

One of the most common ways to generate passive income is through digital products such as e-books, online courses, and downloadable resources. For instance, if you have expertise in a particular subject, you can create an online course that provides valuable information to your audience. Once the course is produced and hosted on a platform, it can be sold repeatedly with little to no additional effort. This not only builds your credibility as an expert but also creates a reliable income stream that works for you while you focus on other aspects of your business or spend time with your family.

Affiliate marketing is another effective passive income strategy that can benefit home-based entrepreneurs. By promoting products or services that align with your niche, you can earn commissions on sales generated through your referral links. This method is particularly useful for bloggers and social media influencers who can integrate affiliate promotions into their content seamlessly. As your audience grows, so does your potential for income, allowing you to leverage your existing platforms without overwhelming your schedule with additional work.

Creating physical products to sell online, such as handmade goods or curated items, can also lead to passive income. With the rise of e-commerce platforms like Etsy or Amazon Handmade, entrepreneurs can set up shops that operate independently. Once the initial effort of creating and listing your products is complete, you can enjoy the benefits of sales while you continue to focus on other projects. By automating aspects of your business, such as inventory management and shipping through fulfillment services, you can maximize your time and increase your profitability.

Finally, consider the power of investing in real estate or dividend-yielding stocks as a long-term passive income strategy. While these options may require a significant upfront investment, they can provide a steady stream of income with relatively low ongoing effort. For those looking to diversify their income sources beyond their kitchen table business, exploring these avenues can lead to greater financial stability and security. By understanding and implementing various passive income strategies, you can create a thriving e-business that aligns with your lifestyle and goals, all from the comfort of your home.

Affiliate Marketing Strategies

Affiliate marketing is a powerful strategy that allows you to generate income by promoting products or services from other companies. This approach is particularly beneficial for home-based entrepreneurs, as it requires minimal startup costs and can be integrated seamlessly into your existing online presence. By leveraging your passion and expertise, you can select affiliate products that resonate with your audience and align with your business niche, creating a win-win situation for both you and your partners.

To succeed in affiliate marketing, it's essential to choose the right products or services to promote. Focus on items that you genuinely believe in and that offer value to your audience. For instance, if you are involved in the Kindle Boom niche, consider promoting e-books, writing tools, or online courses that help aspiring authors navigate the publishing world. By selecting products that enhance the lives of your audience, you build trust and credibility, which can lead to higher conversion rates and increased sales.

Another effective strategy is to create high-quality content that naturally incorporates your affiliate links. This can take the form of blog posts, video tutorials, or social media updates. For example, you might write a blog post about productivity hacks for home business owners and include links to tools and resources that can help them work more efficiently. This approach not only provides valuable information but also drives traffic to your affiliate offers, maximizing your earning potential.

Building an engaged audience is crucial for successful affiliate marketing. Utilize social media platforms to connect with like-minded individuals and share your expertise. Participate in relevant online communities, such as forums or Facebook groups focused on home-based entrepreneurship. By nurturing relationships and providing value, you can establish yourself as an authority in your niche, which can significantly boost your affiliate marketing efforts.

Finally, tracking and analyzing your performance is vital for refining your affiliate marketing strategies. Use analytics tools to monitor which products generate the most interest and sales. This data will help you understand your audience's preferences and enable you to adjust your marketing approach accordingly. By continuously optimizing your affiliate marketing efforts, you can create a sustainable income stream that complements your home-based business, allowing you to thrive in the digital marketplace.

Investing in Digital Products

Investing in digital products is a strategic move for anyone looking to turn their passion into a sustainable e-business from the comfort of their kitchen table. Digital products encompass a wide range of offerings, including e-books, online courses, software, stock photos, digital art, and printables. These products have gained popularity due to their low overhead costs and the ability to reach a global audience. For aspiring entrepreneurs, understanding how to create and market digital products can be a game changer, paving the way for a flexible and profitable business model.

Creating high-quality digital products begins with identifying a niche that aligns with your passion and expertise. This is particularly important for those transitioning from traditional employment to running a business from home. Researching market demand and audience needs can help you pinpoint what type of digital product will resonate with potential customers. Utilizing tools such as keyword research and social media insights can provide valuable information about trending topics and gaps in the market, ensuring that your product has a competitive edge.

Once you have identified your niche and product, the next step is to focus on production. This process often involves leveraging various digital platforms and tools to create your offering. For instance, if you're crafting an online course, platforms like Teachable or Thinkific can provide the necessary infrastructure. If you're producing e-books, software like Canva or Adobe InDesign can help you design professional layouts. Ensuring that your product is visually appealing and user-friendly is crucial, as first impressions can significantly impact sales.

Marketing your digital products effectively is another vital component of success. Utilizing digital marketing strategies such as email marketing, social media campaigns, and search engine optimization can help you reach your target audience. Building an online presence through a blog or a dedicated website can also enhance your visibility and credibility. Additionally, consider offering free samples or mini-courses to entice potential customers, showcasing the value of your product and encouraging them to make a purchase.

Finally, focusing on customer feedback and continuous improvement is essential for long-term success in the digital product space. After launching your product, actively seek testimonials and reviews to understand customer satisfaction and areas for enhancement. This feedback loop can guide future product iterations or inspire new offerings. By staying engaged with your audience and adapting to their needs, you can build a loyal customer base, ultimately leading to sustained passive income and growth for your kitchen table business.

Chapter 9: Crafting and Selling Handmade Goods Online

Identifying Profitable Handmade Products

Identifying profitable handmade products involves a blend of creativity, market research, and an understanding of consumer trends. Start by exploring your own skills and interests. What crafts or handmade goods do you enjoy creating? Whether it's jewelry, candles, home décor, or personalized gifts, your passion will drive your business. This personal touch not only enhances the authenticity of your products but also sets you apart in a crowded marketplace. Consider how your unique skills can meet the needs or desires of potential customers.

Next, research current market trends to identify what is selling well. Utilize online platforms like Etsy, Pinterest, and social media to observe popular items and emerging trends in the handmade space. Take note of seasonal products, such as holiday decorations or summer accessories, as these can provide lucrative opportunities. Additionally, pay attention to customer feedback and reviews to understand what buyers appreciate and what they feel is missing in the market. This insight can guide your product development and help you create items that resonate with consumers.

Another key aspect of identifying profitable handmade products is evaluating your competition. Look at similar businesses and analyze their offerings, pricing, and marketing strategies. Identify gaps in their product lines or areas where you can offer something different or of higher quality. Consider your target audience and what specific needs or preferences they have that are not being met. By positioning your products thoughtfully in relation to competitors, you can carve out a niche that attracts customers.

Pricing your handmade products appropriately is crucial for profitability. Take into account the costs of materials, time spent creating each item, and any overhead expenses such as shipping and marketing. Research what similar products are priced at and consider your unique selling proposition. If your items are made from high-quality materials or offer personalized features, you may be able to justify a higher price point. Crafting a pricing strategy that reflects both the value of your work and market expectations will help ensure your business is sustainable.

Finally, leverage digital marketing to promote your handmade products effectively. Use social media platforms to showcase your creations, telling the story behind each piece to engage potential customers. Building an online presence through a user-friendly website or e-commerce platform is essential for reaching a broader audience. Additionally, consider email marketing and content marketing strategies to keep customers informed and interested in your offerings. By combining your unique crafts with smart marketing techniques, you can turn your passion into a profitable handmade business from the comfort of your kitchen table.

Platforms for Selling Your Crafts

When it comes to selling your crafts, choosing the right platform can significantly impact your success. Several online marketplaces cater specifically to handmade goods, providing a built-in audience eager to discover unique creations. Etsy is one of the most popular options, known for its vibrant community of buyers and sellers. It allows artisans to set up their shops easily, list their products, and engage with customers. The platform also offers various tools to help promote your crafts, making it a top choice for those looking to turn their passion into profit from the comfort of their kitchen table.

In addition to Etsy, there are other platforms worth considering. Amazon Handmade is an excellent alternative for those who want to tap into Amazon's vast customer base. It allows sellers to showcase their products while benefiting from the credibility and reach of Amazon. Additionally, platforms like ArtFire and Handmade at Amazon offer similar opportunities, allowing artisans to connect with buyers who appreciate the value of handmade goods. Each of these platforms has its own unique features, fees, and audience demographics, so it's essential to research and choose one that aligns with your business goals.

Social media platforms also serve as powerful tools for selling crafts. Instagram and Facebook not only allow you to showcase your products visually but also enable you to engage with potential customers through comments and direct messages. Creating a business profile on these platforms helps build your brand and fosters community engagement. You can utilize features like Instagram Shopping to link directly to your products, making it easier for interested buyers to make a purchase. Leveraging social media effectively can drive traffic to your online store, increasing your sales potential.

Another option for selling crafts is to establish your own e-commerce website. Platforms like Shopify, WooCommerce, and Big Cartel provide user-friendly interfaces for setting up an online store. Owning your website gives you complete control over branding, product presentation, and customer interactions. Although it may require more initial effort to set up compared to established marketplaces, a dedicated website can lead to higher profit margins and a more personalized shopping experience for your customers. Additionally, having your website allows for better integration of digital marketing strategies, such as email marketing and SEO.

Finally, don't overlook the potential of local sales channels. Farmers' markets, craft fairs, and local boutiques can provide valuable opportunities to sell your crafts directly to customers. These venues not only allow you to showcase your work in person but also help you build relationships within your community. Combining online and offline sales strategies can create a well-rounded approach to your craft business, maximizing your reach and revenue. By exploring various platforms and adapting your sales strategy, you can successfully navigate the world of e-commerce and turn your crafting passion into a profitable venture.

Marketing Your Handmade Business

Marketing your handmade business is a crucial step towards transforming your passion into a profitable venture. Understanding your target audience is the first pillar of effective marketing. As a home-based entrepreneur, you should identify who your ideal customers are and what they value. Conducting market research can help you uncover insights about their preferences, purchasing behaviors, and the platforms they frequent. This information will guide you in tailoring your marketing efforts to resonate with your audience, ensuring that your products stand out in a crowded marketplace.

Once you have a clear understanding of your audience, the next step is to establish a strong online presence. A well-designed website serves as the foundation for your marketing strategy, showcasing your handmade products in an appealing manner. Additionally, leveraging social media platforms can amplify your reach. Platforms like Instagram and Pinterest are particularly effective for visual products, allowing you to engage with potential customers through eye-catching images and relatable content. Regularly posting updates, behind-the-scenes glimpses, and engaging stories can foster a community around your brand, turning followers into loyal customers.

Content marketing plays a pivotal role in attracting and retaining customers. By creating valuable content related to your products, you can position yourself as an expert in your niche. This could include blog posts about the crafting process, tutorials, or even tips on home-based entrepreneurship. Sharing your knowledge not only builds credibility but also drives organic traffic to your website. Incorporating keywords relevant to your handmade goods will enhance your search engine optimization (SEO), making it easier for potential customers to discover your business online.

Email marketing is another powerful tool for handmade business owners. Building an email list allows you to communicate directly with your customers, keeping them informed about new products, promotions, and exclusive offers. Crafting engaging newsletters can help maintain interest and encourage repeat purchases. Personalizing your emails based on customer preferences can further enhance engagement and foster a sense of community among your clientele, making them feel valued and connected to your brand.

Finally, consider collaborating with other small businesses or influencers within your niche. Partnerships can expand your audience and introduce your products to new potential customers. Participating in online marketplaces or craft fairs can also enhance visibility and provide networking opportunities. As you navigate the marketing landscape, remember that authenticity and consistency are key. By staying true to your brand values and maintaining a steady marketing effort, you can successfully promote your handmade business and achieve the financial freedom you desire from your kitchen table.

Chapter 10: Freelancing Essentials for Desk-Free Professionals

Finding Your Freelance Niche

Finding your freelance niche is a crucial step in establishing a successful e-business that aligns with your passions and skills. In a crowded marketplace, identifying a specific area where you can excel not only sets you apart from competitors but also allows you to effectively target your ideal clients. Start by assessing your own interests, experiences, and talents. Consider what tasks you enjoy doing and what skills you possess that could solve problems for others. This self-reflection is the foundation upon which you can build a freelance career that is both fulfilling and profitable.

Once you have a general idea of your strengths, conduct market research to identify gaps in the market. Look at existing services within your areas of interest and evaluate their demand. Platforms like Upwork and Fiverr can provide insights into what services are currently sought after, as well as the rates freelancers are charging. Pay attention to trends in remote work, digital marketing, and e-commerce, especially those that cater to home-based entrepreneurs. This research will help you pinpoint a niche that not only excites you but also has the potential for profitability.

Networking is another essential aspect of finding your freelance niche. Engage with communities related to your interests, whether through online forums, social media groups, or local meetups. Connecting with other freelancers and entrepreneurs can provide valuable feedback and insights into potential niches. Joining professional organizations or attending workshops can also expose you to new ideas and opportunities. These connections may lead to collaborations or referrals that can enhance your visibility in your chosen niche.

Once you've identified your niche, it's time to refine your service offerings. Consider how you can package your skills into unique solutions that appeal to your target audience. For instance, if you're focusing on digital marketing for home-based entrepreneurs, think about offering tailored services such as social media management, content creation, or SEO consulting. Developing a clear value proposition will help communicate the benefits of your services to potential clients, making it easier for them to choose you over competitors.

Finally, don't be afraid to pivot as you grow. The freelance landscape is constantly evolving, and your interests or market demands may change over time. Regularly reassess your niche and be open to adapting your services based on feedback and market trends. By staying flexible and responsive, you can continue to thrive as a freelancer from your kitchen table, ensuring that your business remains both relevant and profitable in the long run.

Building a Portfolio and Brand

Building a portfolio and brand is a crucial step for anyone looking to turn their passion into a profitable e-business from the comfort of their kitchen table. Your portfolio serves as a showcase of your work, experiences, and skills, allowing potential clients or customers to understand what you can offer. Start by compiling samples of your best work, whether that involves writing, design, or products you create. For those in e-commerce or handmade goods, high-quality images of your products coupled with compelling descriptions can make a significant impact. Ensure that your portfolio is visually appealing and easy to navigate, as first impressions matter.

Branding goes hand in hand with creating a portfolio. Your brand is not just your logo or business name; it embodies the essence of what you stand for and how you want to be perceived in the market. Define your unique selling proposition (USP) that sets you apart from competitors. This could be your approach to customer service, the quality of your products, or the values your business supports. Consistency in branding across all platforms—whether it's your website, social media, or even email signatures—helps reinforce your identity and builds trust with your audience.

In the digital age, building an online presence is essential for attracting customers and clients. Utilize social media platforms that align with your target audience to share your work, insights, and values. Engage with your followers by responding to comments, sharing behind-the-scenes content, or hosting live Q&A sessions. Consider starting a blog to showcase your expertise and provide valuable information to your audience, which can help drive traffic to your portfolio. This not only helps in building your brand but also establishes you as an authority in your niche.

Networking is another vital aspect of building your portfolio and brand. Connect with other entrepreneurs, join online communities, and attend virtual events related to your niche. Collaborate with others in your field, whether through guest blogging, joint ventures, or partnerships. These interactions can lead to referrals, broaden your reach, and create opportunities for growth. Remember that building relationships is a two-way street; be willing to provide support and value to others in your network.

Finally, continually update and refine your portfolio and brand as you grow and evolve. As you gain more experience and feedback, make adjustments to better reflect your skills and the needs of your audience. Keep up with industry trends and adapt your branding strategy accordingly. Regularly assess your online presence and make sure it aligns with your current goals and offerings. By committing to ongoing improvement, you will not only attract more clients but also foster a sense of credibility and professionalism that is essential for long-term success in your kitchen table hustle.

Networking for Freelancers

Networking is a crucial aspect of building a successful freelance career, especially for those transitioning from traditional employment to running a business from home. For freelancers, networking opens doors to new opportunities, collaborations, and resources that can significantly impact their growth and success. Unlike conventional corporate environments, where relationships often develop organically, freelancers must proactively create and nurture connections that can lead to potential clients, partnerships, and valuable insights in their respective niches.

One effective way to network is by utilizing online platforms specifically designed for freelancers and entrepreneurs. Websites like LinkedIn, Upwork, and Fiverr not only allow freelancers to showcase their skills but also provide opportunities to connect with others in similar fields. Joining relevant groups and participating in discussions can help freelancers establish their presence and demonstrate their expertise. Additionally, these platforms often feature forums where freelancers can seek advice, share experiences, and collaborate on projects, creating a sense of community that is essential for growth.

Attending industry events, workshops, and webinars is another excellent strategy for building a network. These gatherings offer freelancers the chance to meet potential clients, mentors, and like-minded professionals. For those who may feel intimidated by in-person networking, virtual events can be a more comfortable alternative, allowing participants to engage from the comfort of their homes. By actively participating in discussions and asking questions during these events, freelancers can make lasting impressions and cultivate relationships that could lead to future business opportunities.

Social media also plays a vital role in networking for freelancers. Platforms like Instagram, Twitter, and Facebook enable freelancers to connect with a broader audience and showcase their work. Engaging with followers, sharing valuable content, and collaborating with other creators can significantly increase visibility and attract potential clients. It's important for freelancers to maintain a professional yet approachable online presence, as this can foster trust and encourage potential clients to reach out for services or collaborations.

Finally, nurturing relationships is key to successful networking. Freelancers should not only focus on making initial connections but also work to maintain and strengthen these relationships over time. This can be achieved through regular communication, sharing updates about their work, and offering support to others in their network. By fostering a spirit of collaboration and mutual assistance, freelancers can build a robust network that not only helps them grow their businesses but also enriches their professional lives. Ultimately, effective networking can lead to increased visibility, more clients, and a supportive community that empowers freelancers on their journey from the kitchen table to success.

Chapter 11: Online Coaching and Consulting from Your Kitchen

Defining Your Coaching Niche

Defining your coaching niche is a critical step for anyone looking to turn their passion into a profitable e-business, especially for those who wish to leave the traditional workplace behind. A well-defined niche allows you to tailor your services and marketing efforts to a specific audience, making it easier to attract clients who resonate with your offerings. For aspiring coaches, understanding the unique needs and challenges of your target demographic can provide a solid foundation for building a successful business from your kitchen table.

To begin the process of defining your coaching niche, reflect on your own experiences and expertise. Consider what knowledge or skills you possess that could benefit others. For instance, if you have navigated the complexities of digital marketing or built an e-commerce business from scratch, these are valuable insights that can guide your coaching focus. Identifying your strengths and passions will help you create a coaching framework that feels authentic and engaging, ensuring that you remain motivated and committed to your business.

Next, conduct market research to identify gaps and opportunities within your chosen niche. Explore existing coaching programs and services to see what is already being offered and where you can differentiate yourself. For example, if you specialize in remote business strategies for moms, examine how you can uniquely address their specific needs, such as balancing family responsibilities with business goals. Understanding your competition and the unique value you can provide will help you position yourself effectively in the marketplace.

When defining your niche, it's also essential to consider your ideal client profile. Who are the individuals you want to coach, and what challenges do they face? Create a detailed persona that outlines their demographics, pain points, and aspirations. This clarity will enable you to craft targeted marketing messages and develop coaching programs that resonate deeply with your audience. Whether your focus is on productivity hacks for home business owners or freelancing essentials for desk-free professionals, knowing your audience will enhance your ability to connect and build trust.

Finally, be open to refining your niche as you gain experience and feedback from clients. The coaching landscape is dynamic, and your understanding of your niche may evolve as you interact with your audience and adapt to market demands. Embrace the opportunity to pivot or expand your services based on what you learn. By staying attuned to your clients' needs and industry trends, you can ensure that your coaching business remains relevant and profitable, allowing you to thrive as you work from your kitchen table.

Setting Up Your Coaching Business

Setting up your coaching business requires a clear understanding of your niche and target audience. Begin by identifying the specific area in which you want to offer coaching services. Whether your expertise lies in digital marketing, productivity strategies, or crafting, having a well-defined niche will help you attract the right clients. Take time to research your audience's pain points and aspirations, as this will inform the content and structure of your coaching programs. Consider using surveys or social media to gather insights about what potential clients are looking for in a coach.

Once you have a clear understanding of your niche, it's time to develop your coaching framework. Outline the core elements of your coaching program, including the topics you will cover, the format (one-on-one sessions, group coaching, webinars), and the duration of the program. Creating a structured approach not only helps you stay organized but also provides your clients with clear expectations.

Incorporate different learning modalities, such as video, audio, and written materials, to cater to various learning styles and enhance the overall experience.

Next, establish your online presence. Create a professional website that showcases your coaching services, testimonials, and valuable content related to your niche. Your website should serve as a hub for potential clients to learn about you and your offerings. Additionally, consider leveraging social media platforms to build a community around your coaching brand. Share insights, tips, and personal stories to engage your audience and establish yourself as an authority in your field. This will not only help in attracting clients but also in building trust and rapport with them.

Marketing your coaching business effectively is crucial for its growth. Utilize digital marketing strategies such as email marketing, content marketing, and social media advertising to reach your target audience. Create valuable content that addresses your audience's challenges and showcases your expertise. Offering free resources, such as eBooks or webinars, can also serve as lead magnets to attract potential clients. As your business grows, consider exploring partnerships or collaborations with other entrepreneurs in related niches to expand your reach and enhance your visibility.

Lastly, focus on creating a sustainable business model. Consider implementing different revenue streams, such as online courses, workshops, or membership programs, to diversify your income. This not only provides stability but also allows you to serve clients at various levels of engagement. Regularly evaluate your business performance, seek feedback from clients, and be willing to adapt your offerings based on their needs. By implementing these strategies, you can successfully set up and grow a coaching business that thrives from the comfort of your kitchen table.

Marketing Your Coaching Services

Marketing your coaching services requires a strategic approach that resonates with your target audience. As a home-based entrepreneur, especially in the niche of online coaching, understanding your ideal client is paramount. Start by creating a clear profile of who you want to serve. This includes demographics, pain points, goals, and the specific challenges they face. By knowing your audience intimately, you can tailor your marketing messages and offerings to address their needs effectively, making your services more appealing.

Utilizing social media platforms is essential for promoting your coaching services. Sites like Facebook, Instagram, and LinkedIn not only allow you to showcase your expertise but also provide a space for community building. Regularly post valuable content that highlights your knowledge, such as tips, success stories, and client testimonials. Engaging with your followers through comments and direct messages fosters relationships and builds trust, positioning you as a go-to resource in your niche. Consider live sessions or Q&A segments to further engage your audience and demonstrate your coaching style.

Content marketing is another powerful strategy for marketing your coaching services. By creating a blog or a series of informative articles, you can establish yourself as an authority in your field. Share insights, strategies, and case studies that reflect your coaching approach. This not only boosts your visibility through search engines but also provides potential clients with a taste of what they can expect from your services. Additionally, offering free resources such as eBooks or webinars can entice prospects to subscribe to your mailing list, allowing you to nurture these leads over time.

Email marketing is a crucial component of your marketing strategy. Once you have a list of interested prospects, keep them engaged with regular newsletters that provide value. Share success stories, updates on your coaching services, and exclusive offers. Personalization is key; segment your list based on interests or behaviors to ensure that your messages resonate with each recipient. This targeted approach increases the likelihood of converting leads into clients, as people are more likely to respond to content that speaks directly to their needs and aspirations.

Finally, consider leveraging partnerships and collaborations to expand your reach. Connect with other entrepreneurs in related niches, such as digital marketing or e-commerce, to cross-promote each other's services. Guest blogging, joint webinars, or co-hosted events can introduce your coaching services to new audiences while also providing added value. Building a network of supportive peers not only enhances your credibility but also creates opportunities for referrals, ultimately helping you grow your business from the comfort of your kitchen table.

Chapter 12: Virtual Assistants: Building a Business from Home

Skills Required for Virtual Assistance

Virtual assistance has emerged as a popular avenue for those looking to transition from traditional employment to running a business from home. To succeed as a virtual assistant, one must possess a diverse set of skills that cater to various client needs. First and foremost, strong organizational skills are essential. Virtual assistants often juggle multiple tasks, schedules, and deadlines simultaneously. The ability to prioritize tasks effectively, manage time well, and maintain an organized workflow ensures that projects are completed efficiently and clients remain satisfied.

Another critical skill is communication. As a virtual assistant, you will be interacting with clients and team members primarily through emails, chat, and video calls. Clear and concise communication is paramount to avoid misunderstandings and to foster a productive work environment. Additionally, being an active listener is crucial; understanding a client's needs and responding appropriately can build trust and strengthen professional relationships. A virtual assistant must also be adaptable in their communication style to suit varied clients and projects.

Technical proficiency is also a significant asset for virtual assistants. Familiarity with various software applications, such as project management tools, spreadsheets, and communication platforms, can enhance productivity. Proficiency in digital marketing tools, customer relationship management (CRM) systems, and basic graphic design software can set a virtual assistant apart in a competitive market. As technology continues to evolve, a commitment to ongoing learning and adaptation is vital for staying relevant in this field.

Problem-solving skills are equally important. Virtual assistants often encounter unexpected challenges, whether it's a last-minute request from a client or a technical issue that disrupts workflow. The ability to think critically, assess situations, and develop practical solutions quickly can prevent minor issues from escalating. Cultivating a proactive approach to problem-solving demonstrates reliability and resourcefulness, traits that clients highly value.

Finally, a successful virtual assistant should possess a strong sense of self-discipline and motivation. Working from home presents unique challenges, including distractions and the temptation to procrastinate. Maintaining focus and producing consistent, high-quality work requires a commitment to one's professional goals. Setting clear boundaries, establishing a dedicated workspace, and implementing productivity hacks can help virtual assistants thrive in their home business environment, ultimately leading to long-term success and growth.

Finding Your First Clients

Finding your first clients can be one of the most daunting tasks for any new entrepreneur, especially when you're transitioning from a traditional job to running a business from your kitchen table. The key is to leverage your existing network while also exploring new avenues to reach potential clients. Start by informing your friends, family, and acquaintances about your new venture. Utilize social media platforms to announce your services and share your passion. Authentic engagement with your personal network can lead to referrals and word-of-mouth recommendations, which are invaluable for building your initial client base.

In addition to tapping into your existing connections, consider joining relevant online communities and forums. Platforms like Facebook groups, LinkedIn, and dedicated forums for your niche are goldmines for networking and finding clients. Participate actively by sharing your expertise, answering questions, and providing value to group members. This will not only help you establish your credibility but also increase your visibility among potential clients who may need your services. Remember, the goal is to build relationships, not just to sell.

Another effective strategy is to offer free or discounted services to your first few clients. This approach allows you to gain valuable experience while simultaneously building your portfolio. As a home-based entrepreneur, showcasing your work is crucial to attracting new clients. Ask satisfied clients for testimonials and permission to display their projects on your website or social media. Positive reviews can significantly influence potential clients' decisions, making them more likely to choose your services over competitors.

Utilizing content marketing can also play a pivotal role in attracting your first clients. Start a blog or create videos related to your niche, providing valuable insights and tips that demonstrate your expertise. This not only positions you as a knowledgeable resource but also helps with search engine optimization, making it easier for potential clients to find you online. Share your content across social media and engage with your audience to create a community around your brand. Consistent content creation can lead to organic traffic and inquiries from clients interested in your services.

Lastly, consider collaborating with other entrepreneurs in your niche or complementary businesses. Joint ventures, guest blogging, or co-hosting webinars can expose you to a broader audience and introduce you to potential clients who may not have found you otherwise. Building partnerships can also offer mutual benefits, such as sharing leads and resources. By diversifying your client acquisition strategies and remaining proactive, you will not only find your first clients but also lay a solid foundation for sustained growth in your kitchen table business.

Setting Your Rates and Services

Setting your rates and services is a crucial step in transforming your passion into a profitable e-business. As you embark on this journey from your kitchen table, it's essential to evaluate the value you bring to your customers. Research similar offerings in your niche to understand the market landscape. This will help you gauge what potential clients are willing to pay and what competitors are charging. Take into account your expertise, the quality of your service or product, and any unique selling points that differentiate you from others in the field.

When determining your rates, consider both fixed and variable costs associated with running your business. Fixed costs may include web hosting, marketing, and any software subscriptions, while variable costs could encompass materials for handmade goods or fees for online platforms. Understanding these costs will help you set prices that ensure profitability while remaining competitive. Additionally, think about your target audience and their budget. For instance, if you are targeting busy moms seeking remote business strategies, consider offering tiered pricing or packages that cater to different financial capabilities.

Service offerings should align with your skills and the needs of your audience. Identify what services will resonate most with your target market. For example, if you excel in digital marketing, you might offer social media management, SEO consultation, or content creation services. Conversely, if you are focused on e-commerce, consider creating product bundles or subscription services that provide ongoing value to customers. Clearly defining your services not only enhances your credibility but also simplifies the decision-making process for potential clients.

It's also vital to stay flexible with your rates and services as you grow. Initial pricing may need adjustment as you gain more experience or as market demands shift. Regularly reassess your offerings and seek feedback from customers to determine if adjustments are necessary. This adaptability will allow you to refine your business model while ensuring that you continue to meet the evolving needs of your clients.

Finally, communicate your value proposition clearly. Use your website, marketing materials, and social media to convey the benefits of your services. Educate potential customers about what they can expect and how your offerings can solve their problems. By effectively marketing your services and justifying your rates, you build trust and credibility, paving the way for sustained growth and success in your kitchen table business venture.

Chapter 13: Blogging for Profit: Monetizing Your Kitchen Table Ideas

Starting Your Blog

Starting a blog can be one of the most effective ways to transition from a traditional job to running a business from your kitchen table. It serves as a platform to share your passion, establish your expertise, and build a community around your interests. To begin, select a niche that resonates with you and aligns with your business goals. Whether you're focusing on e-commerce tips, digital marketing strategies, or freelance essentials, having a clear focus will help you attract the right audience and create content that is both engaging and valuable.

Once you've identified your niche, choose a blogging platform that suits your needs. Popular options include WordPress, Blogger, and Squarespace, each offering various features to help you create a professional-looking site without requiring extensive technical skills. Consider your budget, desired level of customization, and ease of use when making your choice. Remember, your blog will be the face of your brand, so investing time in selecting the right platform is crucial for your long-term success.

Next, create a content plan that outlines the topics you want to cover, the frequency of your posts, and any special series or themes. This plan will serve as a roadmap, helping you stay organized and consistent in your blogging efforts. Aim to produce high-quality content that addresses the needs and interests of your target audience. Whether it involves sharing personal experiences, offering practical advice, or providing resources, your posts should reflect your unique voice and expertise, fostering a connection with your readers.

Incorporating effective digital marketing strategies will also be essential to promote your blog and drive traffic. Utilize social media platforms, email marketing, and search engine optimization (SEO) techniques to reach a broader audience. Engage with your readers through comments and social media interactions to build a loyal community. Collaborating with other bloggers or influencers in your niche can also expand your reach and introduce your content to new audiences.

Finally, consider ways to monetize your blog to create passive income streams. Explore options such as affiliate marketing, sponsored posts, or creating digital products like e-books and online courses. As your blog grows, you can diversify income sources by offering coaching or consulting services, leveraging your expertise in your niche. By staying focused on your passion and continually providing value to your audience, you can successfully turn your blog into a profitable e-business right from your kitchen table.

Content Creation Strategies

Content creation is the backbone of any successful e-business, especially for those looking to escape the confines of a traditional workplace and thrive from their kitchen tables. The key to effective content creation lies in understanding your target audience and providing them with valuable information that resonates with their needs and aspirations. For those focused on niches like digital marketing for home-based entrepreneurs or crafting and selling handmade goods online, the content should be tailored to address specific challenges and interests within these fields. This targeted approach not only builds credibility but also fosters a loyal community that looks to you for guidance and inspiration.

One effective strategy for content creation is to leverage storytelling. Sharing personal experiences, including the journey of leaving a cubicle job to pursue a passion, can create an emotional connection with your audience. This is particularly relevant for remote business strategies for moms, who often seek relatable content that reflects their unique experiences. By weaving narratives that highlight challenges faced and lessons learned, you can inspire and motivate others who are on a similar path, making your content more engaging and memorable.

In addition to storytelling, incorporating a variety of content formats can enhance engagement and reach. Consider blending articles, videos, podcasts, and social media posts to cater to different preferences. For instance, a tutorial video on creating passive income streams from home can attract viewers who prefer visual learning, while a blog post detailing e-commerce tips for kitchen table startups can provide in-depth information for those who enjoy reading. Diversifying your content not only keeps your audience engaged but also maximizes the chances of reaching a wider audience across different platforms.

Another crucial aspect of content creation is consistency. Establishing a regular posting schedule helps build anticipation among your audience and keeps your brand top of mind. For freelance professionals and online coaches, maintaining a consistent voice and style across all platforms reinforces your brand identity and professionalism. It is essential to create a content calendar that outlines topics, formats, and posting dates. This will streamline your workflow and ensure that you remain focused on your content goals while also allowing for flexibility to adapt to trending topics or audience feedback.

Finally, engaging with your audience is vital for successful content creation. Encourage interaction through comments, social media shares, and feedback requests. This two-way communication not only builds a sense of community but also provides insights into what your audience values most. By actively listening to their needs and preferences, you can refine your content strategy to better serve them. This approach is particularly effective for blogging for profit and virtual assistant services, where understanding client pain points can lead to more targeted and effective content that drives business growth.

Monetization Methods for Bloggers

Monetization for bloggers can take various forms, each offering unique opportunities to turn passion into profit. One of the most common methods is affiliate marketing, where bloggers promote products or services and earn a commission for every sale made through their referral links. This approach is particularly effective for those in niches like digital marketing or e-commerce, as it allows for seamless integration of recommended tools and resources into the content. By selecting affiliate programs that align with their blog's theme and audience interests, bloggers can generate substantial income while providing valuable recommendations.

Another popular method is sponsored content, where brands pay bloggers to create posts that feature their products or services. This strategy works well for bloggers who have built a strong audience and established credibility in their niche. Sponsored posts not only provide financial compensation but also create opportunities for collaboration with brands that can enhance the blogger's content. It's essential for bloggers to maintain transparency with their audience by clearly disclosing sponsored content, as this builds trust and credibility.

Ad revenue is another avenue for monetization, often facilitated through platforms like Google AdSense or Mediavine. By placing ads on their blogs, bloggers can earn money based on clicks or impressions. This method is particularly beneficial for those who attract high traffic to their sites, as the potential for income scales with increased visitor numbers. However, bloggers must balance ad placement to ensure it does not detract from user experience, which is crucial for retaining readership and engagement.

Offering digital products is a highly effective way for bloggers to monetize their expertise. This can include e-books, online courses, or downloadable resources that cater to their audience's needs. For instance, a blogger focusing on productivity hacks could create a comprehensive guide to time management or a series of workshops on boosting efficiency. Digital products not only provide a significant profit margin but also allow for passive income opportunities, as they can be sold repeatedly without the need for ongoing effort.

Finally, membership sites or subscription models can provide a steady stream of income for bloggers. By creating exclusive content or community access for paying members, bloggers can foster a loyal audience willing to invest in their expertise. This method works particularly well for those offering online coaching, consulting, or specialized knowledge, as it not only generates revenue but also cultivates a sense of belonging among members. By diversifying monetization strategies, bloggers can create a sustainable income that supports their kitchen table business ambitions.

Chapter 14: Success Stories and Lessons Learned

Inspiring Kitchen Table Entrepreneurs

In the evolving landscape of entrepreneurship, kitchen table entrepreneurs are emerging as a powerful force, transforming their passions into profitable online ventures. These individuals often start with minimal resources, leveraging their unique skills and interests to create successful businesses from the comfort of their homes. The journey of these entrepreneurs illustrates that with determination, creativity, and the right strategies, anyone can build a thriving e-business while enjoying the flexibility and freedom of remote work.

One of the key characteristics of kitchen table entrepreneurs is their ability to identify niche markets that resonate with their personal experiences and expertise. For instance, moms seeking to balance family life with a fulfilling career have found opportunities in remote business strategies tailored specifically for their needs. By understanding their target audience and crafting products or services that address specific pain points, these entrepreneurs can develop a loyal customer base and differentiate themselves in a competitive market.

Digital marketing plays a vital role in the success of kitchen table startups. Entrepreneurs harness the power of social media, email marketing, and search engine optimization to reach potential customers and build brand awareness. By creating engaging content and utilizing analytics tools, they can refine their marketing strategies and ensure that their message resonates with their audience. Digital marketing not only enhances visibility but also fosters community engagement, allowing entrepreneurs to connect with their customers on a deeper level.

Creating passive income streams is another essential strategy for kitchen table entrepreneurs. By developing digital products such as e-books, online courses, or printables, they can generate income with minimal ongoing effort. This approach not only provides financial stability but also allows entrepreneurs to focus on other aspects of their business, such as product development or customer service. The dream of earning money while sleeping becomes a reality when entrepreneurs leverage their knowledge and skills to create valuable assets that continue to generate revenue over time.

As the landscape of entrepreneurship continues to evolve, kitchen table entrepreneurs serve as an inspiration to those looking to break free from the traditional work model. Their stories demonstrate that success does not require a grand office or significant startup capital; rather, it is about passion, perseverance, and the willingness to learn and adapt. Whether through blogging, freelancing, or e-commerce, these entrepreneurs are paving the way for a new generation of business owners who are ready to embrace the freedom and flexibility of working from their kitchen tables.

Common Pitfalls and How to Avoid Them

Starting an e-business from your kitchen table can be an exciting venture, but it also comes with its own set of challenges. One common pitfall is the lack of a clear business plan. Many entrepreneurs dive in with enthusiasm, driven by passion, but without a roadmap, they can quickly lose direction. To avoid this, take the time to craft a detailed business plan that outlines your goals, target market, marketing strategies, and financial projections. This plan will serve as a guiding document, helping you stay focused and organized as you navigate the ups and downs of entrepreneurship.

Another frequent mistake is underestimating the importance of branding. In the crowded e-business landscape, a strong brand identity can set you apart from the competition. Many home-based entrepreneurs overlook this aspect, opting for a generic logo or a mismatched social media presence. To prevent this, invest time in developing a cohesive brand that reflects your values and resonates with your target audience. This includes creating a recognizable logo, choosing a consistent color palette, and crafting a unique voice for your communications. A well-defined brand can enhance your credibility and foster customer loyalty.

Time management is another critical area where many kitchen table entrepreneurs falter. The flexibility of working from home can easily lead to distractions, making it difficult to maintain productivity. To combat this, establish a structured routine that includes dedicated work hours, breaks, and time for family. Utilize productivity tools and techniques, such as the Pomodoro Technique or time-blocking, to keep yourself on track. By setting boundaries and adhering to a schedule, you can maximize your efficiency and make the most of your working hours.

Marketing is often an area where new entrepreneurs struggle, particularly when it comes to digital marketing strategies. Many underestimate the power of social media, search engine optimization, and email marketing in driving traffic and sales. To avoid falling into this trap, invest time in learning about various digital marketing channels and how to leverage them effectively. Consider taking online courses or attending webinars to enhance your skills. Additionally, experimenting with different marketing tactics and tracking their performance can help you identify what resonates best with your audience.

Finally, neglecting self-care can be a significant pitfall for those running a business from home. The pressure to succeed can lead to burnout, which ultimately affects productivity and creativity. To mitigate this risk, prioritize your well-being by incorporating regular exercise, mindfulness practices, and time for hobbies into your routine. Setting aside time for relaxation and self-reflection can rejuvenate your mind, allowing you to approach your business with renewed energy and perspective. Remember that a healthy work-life balance is essential for sustainable success in your kitchen table hustle.

Celebrating Your Wins

Celebrating your wins is an essential practice for anyone navigating the transition from a traditional job to running a business from your kitchen table. Each victory, regardless of its size, contributes to your overall journey and reinforces your commitment to your entrepreneurial goals. Recognizing and celebrating these accomplishments not only boosts your morale but also serves as a powerful motivator to keep pushing forward. Whether you've completed a significant milestone, acquired a new client, or launched a product, taking time to acknowledge these achievements can invigorate your passion for your business.

One effective way to celebrate your wins is to establish a regular reflection practice. Set aside a specific time each week or month to review your progress. During this reflection period, list out your accomplishments, no matter how small. Did you finally figure out how to optimize your blog for SEO? Did you receive positive feedback from a customer? Each item on your list deserves recognition. This practice not only helps you appreciate your progress but also allows you to identify areas for improvement and set new goals moving forward.

In addition to personal reflection, consider sharing your wins with a supportive community. Engaging with fellow entrepreneurs, whether through online forums, social media groups, or local meetups, provides an opportunity to celebrate together. Sharing your successes can inspire others and create a sense of camaraderie in your entrepreneurial journey. Additionally, receiving encouragement and validation from peers can enhance your confidence and remind you that you are not alone in your business endeavors.

Another powerful way to celebrate your wins is to reward yourself. This doesn't always have to be extravagant; it can be as simple as treating yourself to a favorite snack, taking a moment for self-care, or enjoying a day off to recharge. Establishing a reward system for achieving specific milestones can keep you motivated and eager to reach the next goal. It's crucial to recognize that these rewards are not just treats; they are acknowledgments of your hard work and dedication, reinforcing the positive behavior of striving for success.

Lastly, documenting your journey can be a fulfilling way to celebrate your wins. Consider starting a blog or a journal dedicated to your business experiences. Share your accomplishments, challenges, and the lessons learned along the way. This not only serves as a personal keepsake but can also provide valuable insights to others in similar situations. By reflecting on your journey, you can appreciate how far you've come while also inspiring those who aspire to leave their cubicles behind and pursue their passions from their kitchen tables.

www.ingramcontent.com/pod-product-compliance
Lightning Source LLC
Chambersburg PA
CBHW070312220526
45465CB00004B/1847